Love Songs for Las Vegas

✧✧✧

Suzanne Burns

FUTURECYCLE PRESS

www.futurecycle.org

*Cover artwork, "Neon Boneyard—Las Vegas," by Kory Westerhold;
author photo by the author; cover and interior design by Diane Kistner
(dkistner@futurecycle.org); Gill Sans text and titling*

Published by FutureCycle Press
Lexington, Kentucky, USA

ISBN 978-1-938853-74-6

Contents

Prologue

"Las Vegas is sort of like how God would do it
if he had money."

—Steve Wynn

In a Roadside Diner

On the way to Nevada
it feels right stopping
at a café for Denver omelets
in the kind of town where
everyone remembers Paul Newman

because the head waitress clocks
her shift hours by how many times
she tells the story of the day
he stopped by to eat a Denver omelet
on the way to film a movie, 1971.

As she refills coffee she says
Thank God his movies
weren't all black and white
with those cool blue eyes
          more miraculous
than the lights of Las Vegas,

which she has never seen because
after meeting Paul Newman
how selfish to spend a life
looking for a little more luck.

Las Vegas: Luminous Readers

Elegy to an Elvis Impersonator

"Man, I really like Vegas." —*Elvis Presley*

Without sideburns your profile
could be the profile of an astronaut
in those '60s *Life* magazine spreads,
emphatic good breeding, heroic
the way firemen once rescued
kittens from every tree

before the real Elvis competed
with Tom Jones, who sang
about giving flowers to a pussycat
the same year you were born.

You are standing there
not really dead
the way the real Elvis is dead

but not really alive
in your own skin,
for tips forced to bear
your cross of blue rhinestones,
your fake microphone,
your oversized sunglasses
to shield yourself
from the paparazzi
that never hold up their cameras
close to your face without asking.

From 8 Weeks to 8 Months

The Fetal Room at the Bodies Exhibit, Luxor Hotel

What you are about to see
is more evolution
than revolutionary,
as fantastic as Elvis
Viva-Las-Vegas-ing down the Strip,

these fingernails shiny
like the sequins he wore
when women lunged for his pelvis
before peanut butter and pills
stopped his over-loved heart.

Nothing would change if he sang hymns
to these little unnamed hearts,
　　　　more red than expected,

or odes to their translucent bones,
the way their arms hug hunched forms,
stop-motion animation under a spotlight

suspended

like the moment every fan felt
Elvis really had left the building
with no time to toss a white scarf
at one of the temporary mothers
who stopped contemplating rattles and cribs
or the glimmer of a bronzed baby shoe
hanging from a rearview mirror
to drive away its own reflection.

Teller's "Shadows"

Does it spoil the illusion
to say there is blood at the end
like most things
that bloom before you?

Maybe a rose is never really a rose
but the deep red shadow
of our own lonely heart
caught for a moment
between beating
and not beating,

between magic
        and not magic,

between the silhouette on the walk
we can never overtake
no matter how much our own bodies bloom,
no matter how many magicians
tell us to look for the thread,
the wand, the two-sided card

and us becoming the thread,
the wand, the two-sided card,

the rose that surrenders its petals
like the promise of a better beauty unfolding.

The trick we fall for every time.

The Titanic Artifact Exhibit

The Luxor Hotel

If my boat ever sinks,
will you visit me?

At least will you please
visit my relics
even though underwater
nothing that makes me human
will translate,
every device that connects
me to you
not even wired to give off

one
last
ping.

I have wrapped my existence
inside my own black box
the way curtains black out
a city that refuses to dream.
A promise it signed up for,
to babysit stragglers
rubbing rabbits' feet near
their lucky slot machines
and the ones who
order dinner at midnight
and the ones who wait for taxis
after the last magician
tucks away his rabbit.

As I tuck my body beside you,
I ponder the porcelain ramekins,
the sheet music, the handful of coins
never spent, tooth powder,
that bottle of champagne,

its cork refusing to pop
then bob across the Atlantic,
unable to lose itself
the way I am unable to drift
towards the current of sleep.

Dessert at the Bacchanal Buffet

Caesar's Palace

More than the meditation
of Pie vs. Cake,
this feels religious
the way all of Las Vegas
flashes itself into fleeting reverence.

Cookies, soufflés, crème brûlées,
the flour and sugar details,
the colors brown and pink,
chocolate-covered strawberries,
glass jars of Chantilly cream

matter less than the permission
this place grants for lavishness

as if we do not come here to be adults
like the advertising says
but to exist as children again
in a wonderland
bordering on the grotesque,

silent vespers to spent cupcake wrappers,
innumerable sweet morsels photographed

so back home we can try to remember
that secret aspect inside all of us
spectacular enough to deserve this.

View from the Mix Bar, Mandalay Bay 43rd Floor

"Las Vegas looks the way you'd imagine heaven
must look like at night."
                                    —Chuck Palahniuk

Straight to the top we sip drinks
and watch the airport
make birds of us all while tonight
we catalog the golden feather show.

City birds fly giddy among fast
black dashes of Vegas bats
who spend each evening
courting the Luxor Hotel light,
a skyward beam made
to commemorate the real
among the rest of us.

The Neon Boneyard

You can look but please don't touch,
as we hear stories
of Sammy Davis Jr.,
the first Black man
to perform at the Sands,

the rise and fall of the Stardust,

an "H" from the Sahara sign
lounging, half-buried,
on its side like an afterthought

that once glowed
in eternal silver sunshine
when Louis Prima sang
about having no bananas
and nobody could imagine
shutting off the light.

Showgirls

They come in twos.

Part of Noah's menagerie,
a different kind of flood story,
the narrative arc of local girls
who pretend to be showgirls
for dollar tips.

Some have feathers.
Some don't bother with feathers.

They treat everyone
like an easy mark,
two blondes more
yellow than champagne,
more bottle than salon,
like the kits we used in high school
to pretend to be anyone but us—

maybe Jean Seberg wearing
a *Herald Tribune* T-shirt,
maybe Courtney Love kissing
Kurt on the cover of *Sassy* magazine—
but never a showgirl

with or without feathers

in the kind of town where
local girls found love at county fairs
with boys who got thrown from bulls
or dirt-biked their way
into emergency rooms,

all of our fake blonde concern
trailing after them
with no idea that spotlight
could ever shine on us.

Frank and Mia

July 19, 1966, a photo at the Hard Rock Café

There is always deception in cake
frosted to emulate a bride
who can never manage to think
her way past that first bite
smashed in her face.

Every woman pretends to wed Sinatra:
                              the idol
                              the dream date

the man who knows when a bride tosses her bouquet
she expects the catcher to return
all her lilies unscathed

or return her husband the first time
he wanders past the expanse of their vows

forgetting how that white dress once sliced
a paradise of flour and sugar into hopeful shapes
with a belief she would wait an eternity
to hand him a perfect plate.

For the Man Who Runs the Liberace Exhibit

The Cosmopolitan Hotel

This town turns everything into a gamble
and my bet's on you
as we talk like childhood friends
about wanting to stroke
Liberace's furry jeweled suits,
all the crystals, inseams threaded
in real gold, the pink lapels
his brother George must have worried
revealed too much behind closed doors.

You become my art installation
with your Cleopatra eyes, dust of gold
glittering down your forehead
holding its own, a darker Candy Darling
more alluring than every feather
on every showgirl combined,
a breathing artifact who speaks
of always respecting the clothes,

but I hope
before the doors close
you reach a demure foot
inside one of his boots
to see how it feels
walking this earth
        just once
with diamond soles.

The Bodies Exhibit

The Luxor Hotel

My body wants to meet your body
in a way that can only happen at night
when everyone's drunkenness
      has rocked them to sleep.

This city is nothing but a giant crib,
and only you and I
have never bought into lullabies.

Brahms would have loved
the whiskey, gin, rum of this place
but I want to meet you,
      see-through and brave
with all the lights on.

Forget about the romance of secrets
lodged between sheets,
in deep folds of skin.
I adore the dusty collapsing
of your left lung,
your awkward yellow spleen,
the space between your legs
curved like a question mark.

You do not need to bring me flowers
because your heart is posing for me
freely, my red and blue Valentine.

Look at those ribs, your bony xylophone
waiting for the music of my fingers,
the bow of your body so broken
I can't help but long to catch you.

Sleeping Under the Big Piece

The Titanic Artifact Exhibit at the Luxor Hotel

It would at least make more sense
to be sleeping beneath
the vast relic shining
under the gallery light
      almost like silver
      almost like glass.

Star-struck, I want to ask
the Titanic Big Piece
for its autograph
or how it feels sharing space
with a 24-hour Starbucks.

This place puts every disaster on display
as if both mobsters and shipwrecks,
for attention, fill themselves with holes.

I wonder in our hotel
if I am the only one awake,
the only one who remembers
the passengers' last words,
the stopped watch, the impermanent
empathy
drowning our room
as I toss and turn in time
to your body's discernible pitch.

Ode to Aubrey

Your face on the side of a bus
circles the strip
like a tan and blonde comet
trying not to burn out in orbit.

You are a celestial moment,
all pink lips and the kind of body
with no bad side
no matter how far you contort
your g-string to catch the best lighting.

The ad guarantees you in person.
You will be you.
You will dance.
You will take a bubble bath

(you will bring your own bubbles)

and I hope that is all you have to do,
someone's small-town girl turned myth
with the kind of cleavage
you could balance the world on
if you only knew how to ask.

Mark at the Mandarin Oriental Hotel

Do you get tired of the city
pulsing its emphatic rainbow
across your face as you bartend
on the 23rd floor,

almost floating among the Vegas clouds
if there were any clouds?

In front of us you line up
a tray of olives, mixed nuts,
a smile that shows all its teeth.

No one has smiled at us in a week,
and I want to ask you how to stay
human among the supernatural sheen,
the whole city reflecting back on itself.

Reflecting on your billboard
of crisp white teeth.
Reflecting in the cherry sinking
to the bottom of my drink,
the glass you brought back
after I forgot to eat
the fleeting sweet bite
you took the time
to put within my reach.

Dancing on the Rio Rooftop

with you feels like crashing a party
in high school where people like us
were given the wrong directions

to the kegger,
    the hot tub,
        the condo.
The one with all the free pizza.
The one with the LSD.
The one with the B-list celebrity
in town to visit his father

while we sat at home
with our overly opposable thumbs,
trying to hitch a ride.

Las Vegas In-and-Out

The first time we ate
double-doubles
under an umbrella outside,
we were one-day married,

driving towards a new life
too full of hope to spy
the coming change of tides.

One-day married
with our best feet forward,
our shoulders poised
to turn the wheel of beginnings,
while our shakes melted
in the sun—too hot
for us to keep up—
so we pretended to cry
over spilled milk years before
so many busted axles
gave us something to cry about.

Nevada Quintet

For the Man Who Pretended He Didn't Want Dessert at the Eldorado Buffet

Reno, Nevada

You are a man abundant in his bones
with your thick arms of tattoos
and a *Penthouse* magazine
bought in the lobby now
secure under your left arm

who meets my face with apology
for wanting too much
because everything here feels
like too much
as if the harsh life
we are all accustomed to
lets go its mortal grip
and grants us permission
to dance near the cheesecake with delight.

I want to tell you
this is no place for shame
as I sign the cross near
a tray of pie and hope
this is another one of those sins
we can swallow into forgiveness.

The Box of Hugs

On a side street in Reno, Nevada

Behind the Silver Legacy
on a side street tourists
never walk down, their route
divined by the promise
of a future gilded
in a royal flush,

sits a large box wrapped
to look like a red present
topped with a red bow.

A card pinned to its side says,
"I am a box of hugs."

You look for the hidden camera
while I scan the other side
of the narrow street
for a box of kisses,

neither of us willing to step closer,
undo the crushed velvet bow
to reveal whether an object
with more promise
than all the city slots combined
could ever be real.

The Symphony Conductor Speaks of Brothels at the Mizpah Hotel

Tonopah, Nevada

While I order a hot fudge sundae,
an anachronism in this old saloon—
though I have spent my life
feeling out of place—
a conductor, symphonies his specialty,
buys my husband drinks.

(Men who buy other men drinks
never buy women hot fudge sundaes.)

The fudge melts my ice cream
over the edge of its silver dish
as if something this sweet in the desert
could never be contained,

while the conductor speaks of art
but says, "ahh-rt,"
his European upbringing now used
to elevate any vowel in sight.

There is "ahh-rt" in the brothels,
the pillared trailers where women
hand out menus for men
to choose from like the whole idea
of sex for money is a treat
more noble than any dessert.

Rock Hunting Near Area 51

Extraterrestrial Highway, Nevada

You take pictures of me,
bent towards the great
cracked earth looking
for white rocks,
as if every angle
will become a photo-op,

as if I posses
no bad angles,
like you get to escort
your own private movie star
across this brown expanse.

Away from home
I always forage for white rocks,
a moveable handful of talismans
to guide us back to where
we started from
in case all those pictures
only you might find pretty
get lost in the motion
of every wrong turn.

To the Waitress at the Silver State Restaurant Who Has Left for Minnesota By Now

Ely, Nevada

You were almost gone in February
when I paid the check and asked
for a piece of pie for the road.

You met a bull rider online,
62 years old, soon
your first time in a plane.

Did the takeoff frighten you,
or did those big wings
make you anxious to fly
into the arms of your new life?

Did you train Maria in back
on how to make all the pies
you proudly made from scratch?

Are her crusts as golden,
her meringues beaten
to a perfect pitch,
while you forget
to send postcards to a town
you finally left, that knows
there's no use missing someone
who gives away
her secret recipes
to anyone that asks?

Epilogue

At a Pawn Shop in Reno

N. Virginia Street

Four bracelets from Tiffany
make four silver circles,
four objects with no beginning
and no end, or four premature endings
in a purgatory, from clasp to clasp,
of eternal return.
But what did Nietzsche understand
of fine jewelry or pawn shops,
or the four silver hearts stamped,
"Please return to Tiffany?"
And where is the man we all hoped
the 5th Avenue flagship store
would deploy to the middle
of a Reno city street
to collect and curate
an army of fallen hearts,
carry home the infinite burden
of fusing all the broken pieces
back together,
each silver fissure too small to see,
each insurmountable longing
to again be whole.

About FutureCycle Press

FutureCycle Press is dedicated to publishing lasting English-language poetry books, chapbooks, and anthologies in both print-on-demand and Kindle ebook formats. Founded in 2007 by long-time independent editor/publishers and partners Diane Kistner and Robert S. King, the press incorporated as a nonprofit in 2012. A number of our editors are distinguished poets and writers in their own right, and we have been actively involved in the small press movement going back to the early seventies.

The FutureCycle Poetry Book Prize and honorarium is awarded annually for the best full-length volume of poetry we publish in a calendar year. Introduced in 2013, our Good Works projects are anthologies devoted to issues of universal significance, with all proceeds donated to a related worthy cause. Our Selected Poems series highlights contemporary poets with a substantial body of work to their credit; with this series we strive to resurrect work that has had limited distribution and is now out of print.

We are dedicated to giving all of the authors we publish the care their work deserves, making our catalog of titles the most diverse and distinguished it can be, and paying forward any earnings to fund more great books.

We've learned a few things about independent publishing over the years. We've also evolved a unique, resilient publishing model that allows us to focus mainly on vetting and preserving for posterity the most books of exceptional quality without becoming overwhelmed with bookkeeping and mailing, fundraising activities, or taxing editorial and production "bubbles." To find out more about what we are doing, come see us at www.futurecycle.org.

www.ingramcontent.com/pod-product-compliance
Lightning Source LLC
Chambersburg PA
CBHW070117070426
42448CB00040B/3120